Freedom From Fear

Selected Stories from *Living with the Himalayan Masters*

by Swami Rama

Also by Swami Rama

The Royal Path: Practical Lessons on Yoga
A Practical Guide to Holistic Health
Celestial Song/Gobind Geet
Choosing a Path
Exercises for Joints and Glands
Fearless Living: Yoga and Faith
Happiness Is Your Creation
Living with the Himalayan Masters
Love and Family Life
Love Whispers
Meditation and Its Practice
Path of Fire and Light
Path of Fire and Light, Volume 2
Perennial Psychology of the Bhagavad Gita
Science of Breath
Spirituality: Transformation Within & Without
Swami Rama Gift Book Set
The Art of Joyful Living
The Royal Path: Practical Lessons on Yoga
Yoga and Psychotherapy

FREEDOM From FEAR

Collected Stories by

SWAMI RAMA

WWW.HIMALAYANINSTITUTE.IN

Himalayan Institute India
A-43, Second Floor, Sector 7
Noida-201301 (U.P.) India
Phone: 0120-4247856/57
Email: hipress@himalayaninstitute.in

www.HimalayanInstitute.in

Cover design by Cheri Knuth
Creative direction and design by Cheri Knuth

The paper used in this publication meets the minimum requirements of American National Standard for Information Sciences—Permanence of Paper for printed Library Materials, ANSI Z39.48-1984.

Library of Congress Cataloging-in-Publication Data

Rama, Swami
Freedom From Fear
ISBN: 0-89389-229-7
1.Yoga. I. Title

Fear is the greatest of all foes.

It is a devil residing within.

Fearlessness is the first rung on

the ladder of freedom.

About the Swami Rama Book Series

Yogi, spiritual adept, teacher, author, and founder of the Himalayan Institute, Swami Rama brought health, peace and happiness to the lives of tens of thousands. The essence of his profound yet simple teachings continues to inspire and direct the lives of sincere seekers around the world. *Freedom From Fear* is a selection of stories from his classic work, *Living With the Himalayan Masters.*

Table of Contents

HOW CAN YOU LOVE
SOMETHING WHEN YOU
ARE UNDER THE
INFLUENCE OF FEAR?

Fear of Snakes

Let me tell you about my fear. In my young age I was usually fearless. I could cross the swollen Ganges River and go into the forest without the slightest fear of tigers—but I was always very much afraid of snakes. I have had many encounters with snakes, but I concealed my fear from everyone, even my master.

Once, in September of 1939, my master and I came down to Rishikesh. We were on the way to Virbhadra, and camped at a spot where my ashram stands today. Early in the morning we took our bath in the Ganges and sat down on its bank for meditation. By that time I had already formed the habit of sitting for two or three hours without a break. It was about seven-thirty when I opened my eyes—and saw that I was face to face with a cobra. The lower half of its body was coiled on the ground, and the upper half was raised. It was sitting very still, about two feet in front of me, looking at me. I was terrified, and immediately closed my eyes again. I did not know what to do. After a few seconds, when I opened my eyes again and found that it had not moved, I jumped up quickly and ran away.

After running for a few yards I looked back and saw that the cobra was just starting to crawl back toward the bushes.

I went back to my master and explained what had happened. He smiled and told me that it is natural for any living creature to be in a state of meditation near someone who is in deep meditation.

Another time, after experiencing many kinds of training, I had another frightening experience with snakes. One cold rainy evening I went to a temple to ask for shelter. At first they said, "If you are a swami, why do you need shelter?" But then a lady came from the temple and said, "Come with me. I will give you shelter." The woman took me inside a small six-foot-square thatched hut and told me to stay there. Then she left. I had only a deerskin on which to sit, a shawl, and a loin-cloth. There was no light in the hut, but I could dimly see from the light that came through the entrance. After a few minutes I saw a cobra crawling in front of me—and then another one at my side. Soon I was aware that there were several cobras in the room. I realized that I had come to a snake's temple! It was a very dangerous situation, and I was afraid. The woman wanted to test whether I was a genuine swami or not, and I was actually just learning to be a swami. I was very much afraid–but I thought, "If I run away at night, where could I go? And if I do leave, that woman will never give alms to swamis in the future." I decided, "I will remain here. Even if I die, at least the principles of renunciation will not have been found wanting."

Then I thought, "That woman does not appear to be enlightened, and yet she can come into this hut. So why can't I remain here without being harmed?"

Remembering my master's words, I said to myself, "If I sit still, what will the cobras do to me? I have nothing that they want." I sat there the whole night watching, and the only thing I lost was my meditation. I could only meditate on the cobras.

Despite these two experiences, however, my fear of snakes continued. As a young swami many people, even high government officials, came and bowed before me and I blessed them. But within me was an obsessive fear of snakes. I would teach the Brahma Sutras, the philosophy of fearlessness, to my students, but fear was there inside me. I tried my best to remove the fear by intellectualizing it, but the more I tried, the stronger the fear became. It became so strong that it started creating problems. With any sudden noise the thought of snakes would come into my mind. When I sat for meditation I would often open my eyes and look about. Wherever I went I would look for a snake. Finally I said to myself, "You must remove this fear even if you die in the process. It is not good for your growth. How can you lead people who love, respect, and depend on you? You have this fear and yet you are guiding people—you are a hypocrite."

I went to my master and I said, "Sir?" He said, "I know what you want. You are afraid of snakes."

"If you knew, why didn't you tell me how to get rid of that fear?" I asked. He said, "Why should I tell you? You should ask me. Why did you try to hide this fear from me?" I had never kept any secret from him, but somehow I did not tell him about this fear.

Then he took me to the forest and said, "We are observing silence starting tomorrow at dawn. At three-thirty in the morning you will get up and collect leaves and wild flowers for a special worship that we will do."

The next morning I found a big heap of leaves. As I picked up the heap in the darkness, I realized that there was a cobra in it. It was in my hand, and there was no escape. I did not know what to do. I was so frightened that I was on the verge of collapsing. My hands were trembling. My master was there and he said, "Bring it to me." I was shaking with fear. He said, "It will not bite you."

The unconscious fear welled up nevertheless. My mind said, "It is death that you are holding in your hand." I believed my master, but my fear was stronger than my belief.

He said, "Why do you not love the snake?"

"Love?" I cried, "How can you love something when you are under the influence of fear?" This is a familiar situation in the world: if you are afraid of a person, you cannot love him. You will be unconsciously afraid of him all the time. The cause of fear grows in the unconscious.

My master said, "Look, it's such a beautiful creature. It roams all over, but look how clean and neat it is. You do not remain clean; you have to take a bath every day. A snake is the cleanest creature in the world."

I said, "It is clean, but it is also dangerous."

He told me, "Man is more unclean and poisonous

than a snake. He can kill and injure others. Each day he projects poison in the form of anger and other negative emotions on those with whom he lives. A snake never does that. A snake bites only in defense."

He went on: "When you are fast asleep, does your finger prick your own eyes? Do your teeth bite your tongue? There is an understanding that all your limbs belong to one body. The day we have a like understanding that all creatures are one, we will not fear any creature."

I continued to hold the snake as he talked, and gradually my fear subsided. I began to think, "If I don't kill snakes, why should a snake kill me? Snakes don't bite anyone without reason. Why should they bite me? I am nobody in particular." My mind gradually began to function normally. Since that experience I have not again been afraid of snakes.

Animals are instinctively very sensitive and are receptive to both hatred and love. If one has no intention to harm animals, they become passive and friendly. Even wild animals would like to associate with human beings. In the valleys of the Himalayas I observed that animals would come near the villages at night and return to the forest early in the morning. They seem to want to be near human beings, but are afraid of the human's violent nature. A human being, with all his selfishness, attachments, and hatred, loses touch with his essential nature and thus frightens the animals, who then attack in self-defense. If a person learns to behave gently with animals, they will not attack him. I often remember the way Valmiki, St. Francis, and Buddha loved animals, and I try to follow their example.

Fear gives birth to insecurity, which creates imbalance in the mind, and this influences one's behavior. If you examine a fear, you will usually find it is based on imagination, but that imagination can create a kind of reality. It is true that fear creates danger, and human beings then must protect themselves from that self-created danger. All of our dreams materialize sooner or later. Thus, it is really fear that invites danger, though we usually think that danger brings on the fear. Fear is the greatest sickness that arises from our imagination. I have seen

IF YOU EXAMINE A FEAR, YOU WILL USUALLY FIND IT IS BASED ON IMAGINATION.

that all fears and confusion can easily be overcome with practical experience.

The first ten commitments of the Yoga Sutras are prerequisites for attaining samadhi—and the first is ahimsa. Ahimsa means non-killing, non-harming, and non-injury. By becoming selfish and egotistical, human beings become insensitive and lose the power of instinct. Properly used, instinct can help you on the path of ahimsa.

In all my years of roaming in the mountains and forests of India I have never heard that any wild animal ever attacked a sadhu, swami, or yogi. These people do not protect themselves from the animals or natural calamities like avalanches. It is inner strength that makes one fearless, and it is the fearless one who transcends individual consciousness and becomes one with the universal consciousness. Who can kill whom? For Atman is eternal, though the body must return to dust sooner or later. This strong faith is enjoyed by all the sages in the lap of the Himalayas.

WE BUILD WALLS
AROUND OURSELVES
AND LOSE TOUCH
WITH OUR OWN
INNER BEING AND
THEN WITH OTHERS.

In a Tiger's Cave

Once I was traveling all alone in Tarai Bhavar toward the mountains in Nepal. I was on my way to Katmandu, which is the capital of Nepal. I walked twenty to thirty miles each day. After sunset I would build a fire, meditate, and then rest. I would begin walking again at four o'clock the next morning and walk until ten o'clock. Then I would sit near water under a tree through the middle part of the day, and travel again from three-thirty until seven in the evening. I walked in my bare feet carrying a blanket, a tiger skin, and a pot of water.

At about six o'clock one evening I became tired and decided to take a short nap in a cave which was about two miles from the nearest road. I spread my blanket on the floor of the small cave because it was a little damp. As soon as I lay down and closed my eyes I was pounced on by three little tiger cubs, who made gentle cries and pawed at my body. They were hungry and thought that I was their mother. They must have been only twelve to fifteen days old. For a few minutes I lay there petting them.

When I sat up, their mother was standing at the entrance to the cave. First I feared that she would rush in and attack me, but then a strong feeling came from within, and I thought, "I have no intention to hurt these cubs. If she leaves the entrance of the cave, I will go out." I picked up my blanket and pot of water. The mother tiger backed off from the entrance and I went out. When I had gone about fifteen yards from the entrance, the mother tiger calmly went in to join her babies.

Such experiences help one to control fear and give a glimpse of the unity that lies between animals and human beings. Animals can easily smell violence and fear. Then they become ferociously defensive. But when animals become friendly they can be very protective and help human beings. One human being may desert another in danger, but animals rarely do so.

The sense of self-preservation is of course strong in all creatures, but animals are more dedicated lovers than human beings. Their friendship can be relied upon. It is unconditional, while relationships between people are full of conditions.

We build walls around ourselves and lose touch with our own inner being and then with others. If the instinctive sensitivity for our relation to others is regained, we can become realized without much effort.

Mistaken for a Ghost

When I was staying in the Nanital forests in the Himalayan foothills I would sometimes come down to a small city at the height of 6,000 feet. People there would chase after me for blessings and advice, as they do with most yogis and swamis.

In order to have time to do my practices I found it necessary to protect myself from visitors. I heard about a British cemetery which was quiet and neatly kept.

Wearing a long white gown made from a blanket to protect myself from the cold, I went to the cemetery to meditate at night.

One night two policemen who were patrolling that area walked through the cemetery, flashing lights here

AMONG ALL

THE FEARS,

THE FEAR

OF DYING

IS DEEPLY

ROOTED

IN THE

HUMAN HEART.

and there looking for vandals. I was sitting in meditation on the broad monument of a British military officer. My whole body, including my head, was covered with the blanket. The policemen flashed their lights in my direction from some distance away and were startled to see a human-like figure covered with a blanket. They went to the police station and told the other officers that they had seen a ghost in the cemetery. This rumor spread all over the city and many people were frightened.

The superintendent of police came to the cemetery the next night with several armed policemen and flashed light on me once again. In that state of meditation I was not aware of them, so I did not stir. They all thought I was a ghost. They drew their revolvers to shoot at me because they wanted to see if bullets would affect a ghost. But the superintendent of police said, "Wait, let us challenge the ghost first. Perhaps it is not a ghost, but some person."

They came closer and surrounded the monument on which I was sitting. But they still could not figure out what was inside the blanket. Then they fired a shot into the air. Somehow I became aware of them and came out of my meditation. I uncovered myself and asked, "Why are you disturbing me here? What is it you want of me?" The superintendent of police, who was British, knew me very well. He apologized for disturbing me and ordered the policemen who patrolled that area to supply me with hot tea each night. Thus the mystery of the ghost was solved.

Mr. Peuce, the superintendent of police, then started visiting me regularly. He wanted to learn meditation from me. One day Mr. Peuce asked me about the nature of fear in man. I said that among all the fears, the fear of dying is deeply rooted in the human heart. The sense of self-preservation leads one to many hallucinations. A human being is constantly haunted by fears. He loses his balance and starts imagining and projecting his ideas the way he wishes. He deepens this process by repeating it again and again. Fear is the greatest enemy of man.

Mr. Peuce was very much afraid of ghosts and wanted to know if I had ever seen one. I said, "I have seen the king of ghosts—and that is man. A man is a ghost as long as he identifies himself with the objects of his mind. The day he becomes aware of his essential nature, his true self, he is free from all fears."

It is of no use to live under the pressure of fear, for there is no joy in being afraid in every step of life. Without encountering the fears, we only strengthen them. On the path of spirituality, fear and sloth are the prime enemies.

The Devil

One evening after my brother disciple and I had walked thirty miles in the mountains, we stopped to rest two miles beyond Kedarnath. I was very tired and soon fell asleep, but my sleep was restless because of my extreme fatigue. It was cold and I did not have a blanket to wrap around me, so I put my hands around my neck to keep warm. I rarely dream. I had dreamt only three or four times in my life, and all of my dreams had come true. That night I dreamt that the devil was choking my throat with strong hands. I felt as though I were suffocating.

When my brother disciple saw my breath rhythm change and realized that I was experiencing considerable discomfort, he came to me and woke me up. I said,

A NEGATIVE MIND IS THE
GREATEST DEVIL THAT RESIDES
WITHIN THE HUMAN BEING.

"Somebody was choking me!" Then he told me that my own hands were choking me.

That which you call the devil is part of you. The myth of the devil and of evil is imposed on us by our ignorance. The human mind is a great magician. It can assume the form of both a devil and a divine being any time it wishes. It can be a great enemy or a great friend, creating either hell or heaven for us. There are many tendencies hidden in the unconscious mind which must be uncovered, faced, and transcended on the path of enlightenment.

Dreaming is a natural state of mind. It is an intermediate state between waking and sleeping. When the senses are prevented from receiving sense perceptions, the mind starts recalling the memories from the unconscious. All the hidden desires also lie in the unconscious, waiting to find their fulfillment. When the senses are not perceiving the objects of the world and the conscious mind is at rest, then recalled memories start coming forward and they are called dreams. Through dreams we can analyze a level of our hidden personality. This analysis is sometimes helpful in curing certain ailments. With the help of meditation we can consciously recall these memories, observe them, analyze them, and resolve them forever.

THROUGH DREAMS WE CAN ANALYZE A LEVEL OF OUR HIDDEN PERSONALITY.

There are various types of dreams. In addition to the painful and pleasant dreams which we ordinarily experience, there are another two categories of dreams. One is a

prophetic dream, and the other is a nightmare. Sometimes prophetic dreams are guiding. Nightmares are the signs of intense agony created by frustrations. They can also occur if someone is overly tired or has bad digestion.

I have never heard anyone claiming to have seen a devil in the daytime. My brother disciple, with the help of a simile, told me, "A rope in darkness can be mistaken for a snake. A mirage in the distance can be mistaken for water. Lack of light is the main cause of such a vision. Does the devil exist? If there is only one existence, which is omnipresent and omniscient, then where is the place for the existence of the devil? Those who are religiously sick believe in the existence of the devil by forgetting the existence of God. A negative mind is the greatest devil that resides within the human being. Transformation of negativity leads toward positive or angelic visions. It is the mind which creates hell and heaven. Fear of the devil is a phobia which needs to be eradicated from the human mind."

From Fear to Faith

Students are many; disciples are few. Many students came to my master and requested, "Please accept me as your disciple." They all showed their faithfulness by serving him, by chanting, by studying, and by practicing. He did not respond. One day he called everyone to him. There were twenty students. He said, "Let's go." Everyone followed him to the bank of the Tungbhadra River in South India. It was in full flood, wide and dangerous. He said, "He who can cross this river is my disciple."

One student said, "Sir, you know I can do it, but I have to go back to finish my work." Another student said, "Sir, I don't know how to swim." I didn't say anything. As soon as he said it, I jumped. He sat down quietly as

FAITH AND DETERMINATION,

THESE TWO ARE THE

ESSENTIAL RUNGS

ON THE LADDER OF

ENLIGHTENMENT.

I crossed the river. It was very wide. There were many crocodiles, and huge logs were rolling with the currents of water, but I was not concerned. My mind was one-pointed on completing the challenge I was given. I loved to be challenged, and I always accepted a challenge joyfully. It was a source of inspiration for me to examine my own strength. Whenever I was tired I would float, and in this way I succeeded in crossing the river.

My master said to the other students, "He didn't say that he was my disciple, but he jumped."

I was close enough to him to know his power. I thought, "He wants his disciples to cross the river. Here I am. I can do it. It's nothing, because he is here. Why can't I do it?" So firm were my faith and determination.

Faith and determination, these two are the essential rungs on the ladder of enlightenment. Without them the word "enlightenment" can be written and spoken, but never realized. Without faith we can attain some degree of intellectual knowledge, but only with faith can we see into the most subtle chambers of our being.

Determination is the power that sees us through all frustrations and obstacles. It helps in building willpower, which is the basis of success within and without. The scriptures say that with the help of sankalpa shakti (the power of determination) nothing is impossible. Behind all great work and all

FAITH AND DETERMINATION ARE THE ESSENTIAL RUNGS ON THE LADDER OF ENLIGHTENMENT.

great leaders of the world stands this shakti. With this power behind him, such a leader says, "I will do it; I have to do it; I have the means to do it." When this power of determination is not interrupted, one inevitably attains the desired goal.

It is said that the devas are the beings who can travel between both the known and the unknown sides of life.

Lost in the Land of Devas

I had heard and read so much about a village called Jñanganj that my desire for visiting it became intense. Many pilgrims have heard about Jñanaganj, but it is rare that someone perseveres enough to reach there. This small community is situated deep within the lap of the Himalayas, on the border between Tibet and Pithora Garh. For eight months of the year one cannot enter or come out of it, but a small community of yogis lives there year round.

These yogis observe silence and spend most of their time in meditation. Small log houses provide shelter, and their main food is potatoes and barley, which they store for the whole year. The community includes Indian, Tibetan, and Nepalese sadhus. There is no other place but this which can be called Jñanganj.

I decided to visit this village and Mount Kailas along with another four renunciates. We went from Almora to Dorhchola to Garbiank, but after several days we lost our way. It was the month of July when the snow melts in the Himalayan mountains. We found glaciers collapsing, blocking the way behind and in front of us. I was accustomed to such sudden calamities, but the other swamis were new to these adventures, and they were very much frightened.

They held me responsible because I was from the

Himalayas. They said, "You should have known better. You are from the mountains. You misguided us. We have no food, the path is blocked, it is very cold. We are dying here."

We were stranded there by the side of an enormous lake, called Rakshastal, which means "Lake of the Devil." Because of the melting snow and avalanches, the water started rising. By the second day everyone was in panic. I said, "We are not ordinary worldly people. We are renunciates. We should die happily. Remember God. Panic is not going to help us."

Everyone started remembering his mantra and praying, but nothing seemed to help. Their faith was tested–but none of them had any. They were afraid of being buried in the snow. I started joking and said, "Suppose you all die: what will be the fate of your institutions, wealth, and followers?" They said, "We may be dying, but first we will see that you die." My jokes and taking the situation lightly made them more angry.

Few people know how to enjoy humor. Most people become very serious in such adverse situations. Humor is an important quality that makes one cheerful in all walks of life. When the poison was given to Socrates, he made a few jokes. When the cup of hemlock was given to him he said, "Can I share a bit of it with the gods?" Then he smiled and said, "Poison has no power to kill a sage, for a sage lives in reality, and reality is eternal." He smiled and took the poison.

I said to these renunciates, "If we have to live and if

we are on the right path, the Lord will protect us. Why should we worry?" It started becoming dark and again snow started falling. Suddenly a man with a long beard wearing a white robe and carrying a lantern appeared before us. He asked, "Have you lost your way?"

"For almost two days we have had nothing to eat, and we do not know how to get out of this place," we replied. He told us to follow him. There had seemed to be no way through that avalanche, but when we followed him we eventually found ourselves on the other side. He showed us the way to a village which was a few miles away and instructed us to pass the night there. He

IF WE ARE ON THE RIGHT PATH, THE LORD WILL PROTECT US.

then suddenly disappeared. We all wondered who he was.

The villagers say that such experiences are not uncommon in this land of devas. These bright beings guide innocent travelers when they lose their way. We stayed in the village that night.

The next day the other four renunciates refused to travel with me. They all turned back. They did not want to go further into the mountains because they feared more dangers. After being given directions by the villagers I went alone toward Jñanganj. One of the sadhus there was kind enough to give me shelter, and I stayed for one and a half months. This place is surrounded by high snowy peaks and is one of the most beautiful places that I have ever seen.

Returning from Jñanganj, I came back by the way that leads to Manasarowar at the foot of Mount Kailas. I met many advanced Indian and Tibetan yogis. For a week I lived in a camp of lamas at the foot of Mount Kailas. I still treasure this experience. I traveled to Garviyauk with a herd of sheep. The shepherds with whom I traveled talked about the beings who guide travelers in the Himalayas. They narrated many such experiences to me.

These beings are called devas, or bright beings. It is said that the devas are the beings who can travel between both the known and unknown sides of life. They can penetrate through physical existence to guide aspirants, and yet they live in the non-physical plane. The devas too have their plane of existence. Esoteric science and occultism talk much about such beings, but modern scientists dismiss this theory, saying that such beings are either fantasies or hallucinations.

Scientists have not yet studied many dimensions of life. They are still studying the brain and its various zones. The aspect of psychology which is termed transpersonal or transcendental psychology is beyond the grasp of modern science. The perennial psychology of the ancients which has been cultivated for centuries is an exact science. It is based on the finest knowledge—intuition. The physical sciences have limitations, and their investigations are only on the gross levels of matter, body, and brain.

Sri Swami Rama

One of the greatest adepts, teachers, writers, and humanitarians of the 20th century, Swami Rama is the founder of the Himalayan Institute. Born in northern India, he was raised from early childhood by a Himalayan sage, Bengali Baba. Under the guidance of his master he traveled from monastery to monastery and studied with a variety of Himalayan saints and sages, including his grandmaster, who lived in a remote region of Tibet. In addition to this intense spiritual training, Swami Rama received higher education in both India and Europe. From 1949 to 1952, he held the prestigious position of Shankaracharya of Karvirpitham in south India. Thereafter, he returned to his master to receive further training at his cave monastery, and in 1969 came to the United States where he founded the Himalayan Institute. His best known work, *Living with the Himalayan Masters,* reveals the many facets of this exceptional adept and demonstrates his embodiment of the living tradition of the East.

THE HIMALAYAN INSTITUTE

GLOBAL HEADQUARTERS (USA)

The main building of the Institute headquarters near Honesdale, Pennsylvania, USA.

FOUNDED IN 1971 BY SWAMI RAMA, the Himalayan Institute has been dedicated to helping people grow physically, mentally, and spiritually by combining the best knowledge of both the East and the West.

Our international headquarters is located on a beautiful 400-acre campus in the rolling hills of the Pocono Mountains of northeastern Pennsylvania, USA. The atmosphere here is one to foster growth, increase inner awareness, and promote calm. Our grounds provide a wonderfully peaceful and healthy setting for our seminars and extended programs. Students from all over the world join us here to attend programs in such diverse areas as hatha yoga, meditation, stress reduction, ayurveda, nutrition, Eastern philosophy, psychology, and other subjects. Whether the programs are for weekend meditation retreats, week-long seminars on spirituality, months-long residential programs, or holistic health services, the attempt here is to provide an environment of gentle inner progress. We invite you to join with us in the ongoing process of personal growth and development.

The Institute is a nonprofit organization. Your membership in the Institute helps to support its programs. Please call or write for information on becoming a member.

PROGRAMS AND SERVICES INCLUDE:

- Himalayan Institute Press
- *Yoga International* magazine
- Seminars and Workshops
- Meditation Retreats
- Yoga Teacher Training
- Self-Transformation Program™
- Residential Programs
- Pancha Karma
- Himalayan Institute Total Health Products and Services
- Spiritual Excursions
- Humanitarian Projects and Community Centers in Africa, India and Mexico

THE HIMALAYAN INSTITUTE PRESS has long been regarded as the resource for holistic living. We publish books that offer practical methods for living harmoniously and achieving inner balance. Our approach addresses the whole person—body, mind and spirit—integrating the latest scientific knowledge with ancient healing and self-development techniques. As such, we offer a wide array of titles on physical and psychological health and well-being, spiritual growth through meditation and other yogic practices, as well as translations of yogic scriptures.

Himalayan Institute Press Titles

Swami Rama

A Practical Guide to Holistic Health ....₹250
Celestial Song: Gobind Geet ....₹295
Choosing a Path ....₹295
Exercises for Joints and Glands ....₹250
Fearless Living: Yoga & Faith ....₹295
Happiness Is Your Creation ....₹250
Living with the Himalayan Masters ....₹395
Love and Family Life ....₹250
Love Whispers ....₹250
Meditation and Its Practice ....₹250
Path of Fire and Light ....₹295
Path of Fire and Light, Volume-2
(A Practical Companion to Volume-1) ....₹295
Perennial Psychology of the Bhagavad Gita ....₹495
Science of Breath ....₹250
Spirituality: Transformation Within & Without ....₹295
Swami Rama Gift Book Set ....₹250
The Art of Joyful Living ....₹295
The Royal Path: Practical Lessons on Yoga ....₹295
Yoga and Psychotherapy ....₹395

Pandit Rajmani Tigunait, PhD

From Death To Birth (Understanding Karma and Reincarnation).......₹295
Himalayan Masters: A Living Tradition..........₹295
Inner Quest: Yoga's Answers to Life's Questions..........₹350
Lighting the Flame of Compassion..........₹250
Sakti Sadhana (Tripura Rahasya)..........₹295
Seven Systems of Indian Philosophy..........₹350
Swami Rama of the Himalayas (Photobiography)..........₹2500
Tantra Unveiled (Seducing the Forces of Matter and Spirit)..........₹295
The Official Biography of Swami Rama of the Himalayas..........₹395
The Power of Mantra & The Mystery of Initiation..........₹295
The Pursuit of Power and Freedom: Katha Upanishad..........₹295
Touched By Fire..........₹395
Why We Fight..........₹195

Books by Other Authors

Common Sense About Uncommon Wisdom..........₹295
Dhruv S. Kaji

Freedom From Stress..........₹350
Phil Nuernberger

God..........₹295
Swami Veda Bharati

Happiness: The Real Medicine..........₹295
Blair Lewis

Healing the Whole Person..........₹295
Swami Ajaya, PhD

Meditation is Boring..₹295
Linda Johnsen

Moving Inward: The Journey to Meditation..₹350
Rolf Sovik, PsyD

Philosophy of Hatha Yoga...₹250
Doug Boyd

Spirit on the Move...₹295
Yoga International

Yoga Psychology (A Practical Guide to Meditation)...........................₹250
Swami Ajaya, PhD

Call or Email to Order Today!

Himalayan Institute India
A-43, Second Floor, Sector 7, Noida – 201301 (U.P.) India
Phone: 0120-4247856/57
Email: hipress@HimalayanInstitute.in
Website: www.HimalayanInstitute.in

Nurture your mind, body, and spirit

Happiness Is Your Creation

Swami Rama as compiled by Pandit Rajmani Tigunait, PhD

Did you ever pause for a moment and realize that you are the creator of your destiny? In Happiness Is Your Creation, Pandit Tigunait gathered the inspirational teachings of his master, the late Swami Rama, on the yogic prescription for happiness. These enriching passages identify the causes of unhappiness and provide direction to remain centered and joyful in everyday life. Learn how to cultivate a positive mind and charge your body and mind through meditation, allowing you to lead a more active and productive life. This motivational book reveals the ancient teachings of self-discipline, self-mastery, and self-realization through yoga and meditation.

Paperback, 136 pages, ₹250 / US $12.95

Fearless Living: Yoga and Faith

Swami Rama

Learn to live without fear–to trust a higher power, a divine purpose. In this collection of anecdotes from the astonishing life of Swami Rama, you will understand that there is a way to move beyond mere faith and into the realm of personal revelation. Through his astonishing life experiences we learn about ego and humility, how to overcome fears that inhibit us, discover sacred places and rituals, and learn the importance of a one-pointed, positive mind. Swami Rama teaches us to see with the eyes of faith and move beyond our self imposed limitations.

Paperback, 160 pages, ₹295 / US $12.95

Call or Email to Order Today!

Himalayan Institute India
A-43, Second Floor, Sector 7, Noida – 201301 (U.P.) India
Phone: 0120-4247856/57 • Email: hipress@HimalayanInstitute.in
Website: www.HimalayanInstitute.in

091211